# life stinks

## A WRY LOOK AT HOPELESSNESS, DESPAIR, & DISASTER

# life stinks

## A WRY LOOK AT HOPELESSNESS, DESPAIR, & DISASTER

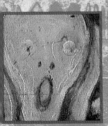

Edited by Ted Mico

Ariel Books

Andrews and McMeel

Kansas City

Frontispiece: Edvard Munch, *Lübeck*, 1903.
Inset: *The Scream* (detail), 1893.

ISBN: 0-8362-3114-7

Library of Congress Catalog Card Number: 94-74179

# Introduction

They couldn't hit an elephant at this dist—

Final words spoken by Union Major General
John Sedgewick as he peered over the
parapet at enemy lines during the 1864
Battle of Spotsylvania

It's sad but true that fate stays in the background most of our lives, showing up only to hand us the fuzzy end of the lollipop. The overwhelming weight of evidence proves that life stinks: If there's a fifty-fifty chance of the toast falling on the floor buttered side down, why does it do so 99 percent of the time? There's no rhyme, no reason, and absolutely no justice. It seems there's only one certainty in life—it's unfair. The diner sitting next to you at the lunch counter will always be served a sandwich that looks fresher and bigger and is surely tastier than yours, especially when both orders are identical. Tollbooth lines, barking dogs, income taxes, bad hair days, Barney, Biosphere *II*—does anyone need more proof of life's pungent aroma?

Only blind optimism could doubt the facts, and, as everyone knows, optimism is the belief

hat everything is beautiful (including what is
ugly) and that everything wrong is actually
right. In real life, the light at the end of the
tunnel is usually an oncoming train. How else
can you explain the fact that just as you are on
your way to the most important job interview
of your life a pigeon will inevitably leave a
comfortable perch on a statue and aim directly
at you? The optimist proclaims that we live in
the best of all possible worlds, and the pes-
simist fears this is true. The realist under-
stands that life's odor is often unpleasant.

The truth of the matter is that we're all
bound by Murphy's Law, which states that
anything that can go wrong, will go wrong,

especially when you least expect it. Just when you think nothing can go awry, Dame Fortune is there quietly slipping lead into her boxing gloves. One minute life is a bowl of cherries, the next you're knocked out cold. But don't take it personally. Take a look at the frustrated and grim faces around you and you'll realize that *life stinks*—not just yours, everyone's.

Optimism is a mania for saying things are well when one is in hell.

—Voltaire

He's turned his life around. He used to be depressed and miserable. Now he's miserable and depressed.

—David Frost

*The object of life is not to be on the side of the majority, but to escape finding oneself in the ranks of the insane.*

—Marcus Aurelius

The fact that life stinks is nothing new. History is littered with examples of fate kicking sand in the face of the blameless. Take, for example, the Bible's trials of Job or the story of Jonah and the whale. Murphy's Law has no respect for virtue or innocence. No matter how many good deeds are done, no matter how many selfless acts are performed, Dame Fortune takes careful aim, freely hurling her slings and arrows at unwary targets.

Even after death, life can still stink, as Christ's loyal apostle Judas Thaddaeus would perhaps agree. For eighteen centuries not a prayer was offered to him, largely because the general public kept confusing him with Christ's betrayer, Judas Iscariot. The Church finally cleared up the misunderstanding by calling him St. Jude and then making him the patron saint of "Hopeless Cases."

The following are some long-forgotten hopeless cases:

In 1799, an American privateer ship called the *Nancy* was chased through Caribbean waters by a British warship. Thomas Briggs, the American skipper, threw the ship's Yankee papers overboard and replaced them with forged Dutch papers in order to avoid being charged with running the British blockade during wartime. The warship eventually caught up with the *Nancy*, and Briggs was taken to Jamaica and tried by the courts. The case was about to be dismissed because of lack of evidence when another British warship, the *Ferret*, arrived in Kingston after having caught a large shark off the coast of Haiti. When the shark was opened, the British discovered all the incriminating papers, which were subsequently used in evidence against Briggs and his crew, who were all sentenced.

In 1792, Dr. Joseph Guillotin visited the Palace of Versailles to discuss the palace locks and to show plans for his new beheading invention—the guillotine. Much to the court's surprise, Louis XVI took an active interest in the meeting. The king even suggested some improvements, such as a blade that could cut at an angle and improve the efficiency of the device. The new modifications worked wonderfully. Six months later, the hapless king discovered just how improved the guillotine mechanism had become. He was executed on January 21, 1793. His wife, Marie Antoinette, met the same fate on October 16, 1793.

When cattle baron James Sutter bought the land between the Sierra Nevada mountains and the Pacific coast, he had no idea what the land contained. On January 24, 1848, one of

his employees, James W. Marshall, discovered a chunk of shiny yellow metal while building a mill. Seven months later, news of the gold strike hit the East Coast, and the first prospectors arrived in February 1849. The so-called forty-niners took over Sutter's land, setting up shantytowns that would later become Sacramento and San Francisco. After seven years, the courts finally ruled that Sutter had

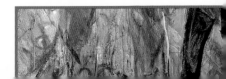

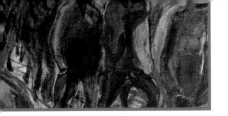

rights to all the land, and the population went wild. They burned his house and furniture, shot his cattle, and murdered his son. Sutter's second son drowned while trying to escape, and the third committed suicide. Yet Sutter became the richest man in America. Not surprisingly under the circumstances, he also went completely mad.

*life stinks*

**O**n October 30, 1883, U.S. Marshall Nate Wilson faced off two outlaws on the main street of Tucson, Arizona. Wilson was famous for three things: charming absent-mindedness, ornate cowboy boots (which were always perfectly polished), and sharp reflexes. As he and the outlaws went for their guns, witnesses could see that the marshall was clearly the faster draw. However, he'd forgotten to remove the leather safety loop around the hammer of his Colt and only realized this tiny aberration *after* his index finger had squeezed the trigger. According to an account in the local paper, Nate Wilson shot himself in the foot, hopped four times on the spot, and was then gunned down by the outlaws, who later stole the marshall's prized boots—still perfectly polished, but now containing a hole.

The Iroquois Theater opened in Chicago in 1903. It was famous throughout the theater community, not so much for the caliber of the actors who performed on its stage, but because it was heralded as the world's first "absolutely fireproof" theater. After just thirty-eight days, the one thousand–capacity theater burned to the ground when an electrical fault caused a chunk of scenery to catch fire.

In 1911, the White Star shipping line announced the world's first "unsinkable" passenger liner: the *Titanic*. The ship began her maiden voyage from Southampton, England, to New York on April 10, 1912. Four days later, at 11:40 P.M., the unthinkable happened to the unsinkable: the *Titanic* struck an iceberg, and fifteen hundred of its passengers went down with the ship. As the thousands of would-be travelers who couldn't get tickets for the trip would testify, missing the boat is not always such a bad thing.

The great escapologist Harry Houdini wriggled out of handcuffs, straitjackets, sealed containers, padlocked chains, and combinations thereof, but even he couldn't escape the grasp of Murphy's Law. After more than twenty-six years of death-defying feats, fate surprised Houdini backstage in 1926. He had always boasted he could take a punch from anyone and had frequently invited members of his audience to take their best shot. On October

31, backstage after a performance, an amateur boxer who'd seen the show took him up on the offer and punched the unsuspecting Houdini in the stomach. Houdini collapsed and coughed up blood but still performed two more nights. On the third day, the blow ultimately caused his untimely death.

In 1926, after traveling twice over Niagara Falls in a barrel, New Zealand daredevil Bobby Leach died after slipping on an orange peel in Christchurch.

In 1944 American bombers dropped their explosive payload on the town of Schufhausen. They hit the target with incredible accuracy— the only problem was, it was the wrong target.

Although Schufhausen sounded like a German town, it was located in Switzerland— U.S. warplanes had successfully bombed a neutral country. This incident led to a World War II saying: "When the Germans bomb, the British run for cover; when the British bomb, the Germans run for cover; when the Americans bomb, *everyone* runs for cover."

During his lifetime, Henri Matisse was revered as the founder of the Fauvist movement and hailed as one of the twentieth century's greatest painters. However, the French artist could have found out exactly how much his art was really appreciated on October 19, 1961. On that day, the Museum of Modern Art accidentally hung Matisse's

*Le Bateau (The Boat)* upside down. The ship, so to speak, capsized along with the museum's reputation. Forty-four days and over 116,000 viewers later, the mistake was finally corrected.

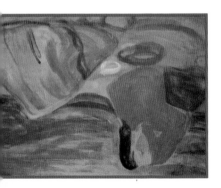

When fate's got it in for you there's no limit to what you may have to put up with.

—Georgette Heyer

The embarrassing thing is that the salad dressing is out-grossing my films.

—Paul Newman

"Know thyself?" If I knew myself, I'd run away.

—Johann Wolfgang von Goethe

We're all in this alone.

—Lily Tomlin

As a confirmed melancholic, I can testify that the best and maybe only antidote for melancholia is *action*. However, like most melancholics, I suffer also from sloth.

—Edward Abbey

The only thing that can stop hair falling is
the floor.

—Will Rogers

In the depths of my heart I can't help being
convinced that my dear fellow men, with a
few exceptions, are worthless.

—Sigmund Freud

It is not true that life is one damn thing
after another—it's one damn thing over and
over.

—Edna St. Vincent Millay

The chief problem about death, incidentally, is the fear that there may be no afterlife—a depressing thought, particularly for those who have bothered to shave. Also, there is the fear that there is an afterlife but no one will know where it's being held.

—Woody Allen

The poor wish to be rich, the rich wish to be happy, the single wish to be married, and the married wish to be dead.

—Ann Landers

A man gazing at the stars is proverbially at
the mercy of the puddles in the road.

—Alexander Smith

The flowers of life are but illusions. How
many fade away and leave no trace; how
few yield any fruit; and the fruit itself, how
rarely does it ripen!

—Johann Wolfgang von Goethe

Even paranoids have real enemies.

—Delmore Schwartz

Sleep is good, death is better; but of course, the best thing would be never to have been born at all.

—Heinrich Heine

## Life Stinks in General

Looked up the elevator shaft to see if the car was coming down. It was.

—Inscription on Harry Edsel Smith's gravestone

Suburbia is where the developer bulldozes out the trees, then names the streets after them.

—Bill Vaughn

**He who laughs has not yet heard the bad news.**

—Bertolt Brecht

There's no remedy and no protection from life's pungent smell. Why is it that the only taxi you ever see when it's raining is the one you see too late—it hits the puddle in front of you at forty miles per hour, drenching you.

Why does the shortest tollbooth line always take the longest time when your car is in it? Or why will the loudest frat-house team always start a volleyball game right next to your blanket on what used to be the quietest part of the beach?

Neither fame, fortune, blue blood, nor even insanity serves as armor against the forces of Murphy, as various celebrities can testify. In 1927, Isadora Duncan was garroted by her own scarf when it got caught in the wheel of a prospective lover's sports car. As Mark Twain said, "Fame is a vapor; popularity an accident; the only earthly certainty is oblivion."

Several years ago in Margate, New Jersey, an unfortunate pallbearer met his end at the local cemetery. It was pouring with rain and the coffin he was carrying was unbelievably heavy, containing the obese Hubert Ross, whose only claim to fame was his legendary ability to consume more hot dogs in ten minutes than any man in New Jersey. As the procession turned to face the grave, the sodden ground around the hole gave way. The pallbearer slipped and fell into the grave, and the heavy coffin fell on top of him, crushing him.

Dick Cavett has the honor of being the only talk-show host who had a guest expire on camera. The guest died of a heart attack just after Cavett had asked him about how to stay in good health. "I suppose it was almost inevitable," the host said later, "that the guest was a health expert."

**D**riving tests have always been a happy hunting ground for failure, but few have achieved this in such brief or spectacular style as Helen Ireland from Auburn, California. She managed to fail her test in one second flat. Mrs. Ireland entered the car, greeted her tester, and started the engine. Sadly, she mistook the accelerator for the clutch peddle, and the car hurtled through the test center wall.

**I**n the late 1960s, a number of U.S. domestic airline flights were hijacked and forced to fly to Cuba. On November 4, 1971, an erstwhile Cuban hijacker named Antonio Visario arrived late at New York's LaGuardia Airport. He had no time to look at the new TV monitors, so he just raced to the nearest gate and got on board the plane. Because the aircraft was a special charter, no one checked his ticket. The plane took off on time, heading south. Twenty minutes into the flight, the hijacker patted his jacket pocket to make sure his firearm was still there, got up, and knocked on the cockpit door. He barged past the flight attendant, took out his gun, and pointed it at the captain's head. "Take this plane to Cuba," he announced. The terrified cockpit crew members looked at one another with amazement. "But sir," the captain replied, "this is a charter plane. We're already going to Cuba!"

The hijacker was so inconsolable over his blunder he was easily overpowered by the cabin crew and was arrested when the plane made an unscheduled stop in Miami.

Two Detroit bank robbers discovered in 1970 that crime doesn't pay, or if it does pay, it pays the wrong person. Having successfully held up a bank, the two thieves raced out to their parked getaway car, only to find it had been stolen.

On August 1, 1985, lifeguards at the New Orleans recreation department threw a party to celebrate the first season in living memory when no one drowned. At least two hundred of the party guests were lifeguards, and there were also four lifeguards on duty. Everything should have gone swimmingly, which is, of course, why it didn't. When the party was over, a party guest was found dead at the bottom of the recreation department pool.

Even the most self-sacrificing people still find their feet inexplicably drawn to cowpats. For example, consider the Dutch veterinary surgeon who only narrowly avoided a prison sentence recently, despite the fact he was just doing his job.

In order to treat a sick cow, the vet attempted to check the animal's internal gases by inserting a plastic tube in its rear and striking a match. The resulting jet of flame set fire to hay bales, then engulfed the entire farm, causing over eighty thousand dollars in damage. Although the cow escaped with shock, the poor vet was arrested and later fined two hundred dollars for irresponsibly starting the fire.

On September 27, 1989, Steven Le and two accomplices attempted to break into a parked pickup truck in Larkspur, California. The truck's owner caught them in the act and chased the gang. Le and one of his friends jumped a tall wire fence and ran. Unfortunately for them, the fence surrounded the property of the San Quentin prison. The suspects were charged with attempted auto theft and trespassing on state property. It's one of the few cases on record when someone tried to break *into* a prison.

## Life Stinks in Business

Success is merely one achievement that covers up a multitude of blunders.

—George Bernard Shaw

I always thought if you worked hard enough and tried hard enough, things would work out. I was wrong.

—Katherine Graham

I was fired from my job at a Howard
Johnson's when somebody asked me the
ice cream flavor of the week and I said,
"Chicken."
                                   —Mike Nichols

Business, as they say, is a tricky business.
One bad roll of the dice in finance can turn the
most successful millionaire into a pauper.
In business, the unexpected application of
Murphy's Law usually results in destitution. Take
the story of a Wall Street tycoon who, in 1928,
gave his alma mater two million dollars to build
a new library. By the time it was finished, the
millionaire had been wiped out by the 1929
stock market crash. The university heads

offered him the job of chief librarian in his own building. He graciously accepted the post.

Not everyone is so lucky. Consider, for example, the film studios involved in the making of *Ishtar* or *Heaven's Gate*, both astounding flops, or the Decca Records employee who turned down the Beatles in 1962, stating, "We don't like their sound. Groups of guitars are on the way out." Or Simon Newcomb, who refused to invest in aviation because "flight by machines heavier than air is unpractical and insignificant, if not utterly impossible." Eighteen months later, the Wright Brothers embarked on their first flight. As you can see here, these poor souls are far from alone:

After making a small fortune from his invention, the telephone, Alexander Graham Bell tried to devote all his time to his one, last ambition: predicting twin births in sheep. The great inventor's experiments were, however, hampered by a never-ending series of annoying interruptions—telephone calls to his Boston laboratory. Eventually, the problem got so bad that Bell was forced to put his own invention out of commission by stuffing it with paper.

In 1948, Mary Sommerville, a pioneer of educational broadcasts, stated, "Television won't last. It's a flash in the pan." While C. P. Scott was a little bit more with the program when he noted, "Television? No good can come of this device. The word is half Greek and half Latin."

Agatha Christie's famous whodunit *The Mousetrap* opened in London in 1952. The play was a great success, so a company called Romulus Films bought the movie rights for a huge sum four years later. The play was a commercial triumph, the author was eminently bankable to audiences throughout the world, and the company was sure to make a fortune from the movie version. There was only one restrictive clause in the contract, stating that the film version of *The Mousetrap* could be released only six months after the show had closed in London. How could their plans go wrong? Unfortunately for Romulus Films, here's how: The play is now in its forty-second successful year and shows no sign of closing. The film version shows no sign of release.

In 1968, the Royal Society for the Prevention of Accidents held its first exhibition in Harrowgate, England. Sadly, the huge display accidentally collapsed, narrowly missing a group of schoolchildren.

On November 8, 1956, Ford Motor Company unveiled its new luxury car to the world—the Edsel. The revolutionary car was a monumental flop with the public. To make matters worse, over half the precious few models that were sold were defective. Among the catalog of complaints were doors and trunks that couldn't be closed, paint that peeled within days, and hubcaps that fit so badly they spun off the wheel. *Time* magazine called it "the wrong car for the wrong market at the wrong time."

There was, however, one advantage to buying a car that was about as popular as a case of anthrax—four years after the first car had rolled off the production line, police had only one report of an Edsel theft.

In the late 1950s, budding soft-drink inventor Richard Keidermacker finally abandoned his ten-year quest for a clear alternative to cola. He'd called his prototypes 4-Up, 5-Up, and 6-Up, but then gave up to work at his father's dry-cleaning store in Paris, Michigan.

In 1962, Arthur Paul Pedrick patented his first invention. Over the next fifteen years, he would patent another 161 inventions, not one of which was ever used commercially. Perhaps his most visionary invention was a device that looked much like a giant peashooter. It was supposed to fire giant snowballs from the polar caps onto the deserts of Africa and thus provide irrigation and food for the world.

In 1991, billionaire Malcolm Forbes paid over $150,000 for a rare bottle of wine from a group of wines known as the Jefferson Collection—so named because the rare vintages were specially made for the third president of the United States. Forbes paid the world-record price to display the bottle in the Jefferson Museum. The exhibitors ignored conventional wine wisdom and displayed the bottle upright and under bright lights. Soon after the display case was installed, the heat from the lights shrunk the cork, which was already more than 150 years old. The cork then plopped into the wine. Overnight, the world's most expensive bottle of wine became the world's most expensive bottle of vinegar.

The U.S. Consumer Product Safety Commission paid for and distributed over eighty thousand buttons in the early 1970s. The button's slogan was "Think Toy Safety." All the buttons had to be recalled because they were found to be dangerously sharp, coated with lead paint, and easy to swallow.

The business farming community around Jeddah, Saudi Arabia, was thrown into confusion in January 1979 after heavy floods. Everyone needed to know when the storms would pass. *The Arab News* issued a bulletin saying, "We regret we are unable to give you the weather. We rely on weather reports from the airport, which is closed because of the weather. Whether we are able to give you the weather tomorrow depends on the weather."

This forecast can be topped only by a 1969 BBC bulletin that bluntly stated, "The weather will be cold." To this was added, "There will be two reasons for this. One is that temperatures will be lower." No one has ever discovered the second reason.

In the early 1980s, microwaves were still regarded with bafflement and suspicion by most of the general public. Unfortunately, a few people had no such qualms, like the housewife who one day decided to shampoo her pet toy poodle. She had just bought a microwave for her kitchen and as she was towel drying her dog, she was struck with the fateful idea: Why not put the pooch into the microwave and dry him faster and with less fuss?

The question was answered one minute after she hit the microwave's start button— the poodle cooked, then exploded. The microwave broke down, but the woman didn't. Despite the tragedy, she sued the manufacturer for not specifically saying in the instruction manual that live animals could not be dried in the microwave. She may have lost her dog, but she won the case.

## Life Stinks in Politics

 There cannot be a crisis next week. My schedule is already full.

—Henry Kissinger

Sometimes at the end of the day when I'm smiling and shaking hands, I want to kick them.

—Richard Nixon

**Politics consists of choosing between the disastrous and the unpalatable.**

—John Kenneth Galbraith

**It is very unfair to expect a politician to live in private up to the statements he makes in public.**

—W. Somerset Maugham

Politicians who complain that life stinks are like captains who complain about the sea. As Oscar Ameringer said, "Politics is the gentle art of getting votes from the poor and campaign funds from the rich, by promising to protect each from the other." Like life itself, politicians always promise what they can't deliver and always deliver what they promise to prevent. Yet because of the spotlight of public scrutiny, when things go wrong in politics, they usually go wrong in spectacular style. Julius Caesar, for example, was warned that his rivals were all back-stabbing malcontents and was told to watch out for the Ides of March (March 15). For Caesar, it was just going to be another day at the Senate. How

was he supposed to know he should have taken such warnings literally? He discovered the truth only when he felt the cold steel of Brutus's dagger between his shoulder blades.

Politics is a minefield of mishaps, yet there are certain people in history who've been lightning rods for disaster. Take, for instance, Abraham Lincoln's eldest son, Robert. First, he witnessed his father's assassination in Box 7 of Ford's Theater on April 14, 1865. Then, sixteen years later, he was standing by President Garfield when Garfield, too, was shot. Finally, Robert was about to join President McKinley at the 1901 Pan-American Exposition when he learned that this president had also been the victim of assassination.

Here are a few more examples of politics and politicians gone wrong:

Everyone knows about Richard Nixon's Checkers speech, his profuse perspiration on TV during the 1960 presidential debate with John F. Kennedy, the Watergate break-in, his swearing on tape, and his ignominious resignation. Yet even when he tried to do something decent, it only accelerated his descent. In April 1969, Nixon decided to honor jazz legend Duke Ellington on his seventieth birthday. Nixon even played "Happy Birthday" on the piano. Ellington kissed the president four times—"One," he told reporters, "for each cheek."

In accordance with the British government's policy of appeasement of Hitler and Nazi aggression during the 1930s, Prime Minister Neville Chamberlain visited Hitler and Mussolini at Hitler's retreat near Munich in 1938. He returned two days later waving a piece of paper and proudly announcing to the British people that there would be "Peace in our time." One year later, Britain declared war. Chamberlain resigned in 1940.

It may have been human weakness that led Democratic presidential hopeful (and married man) Gary Hart to get involved with Donna Rice on a sailboat, but only Murphy's divine intervention could ensure that the couple allowed themselves to be photographed on deck and that the boat was called *Monkey Business*. Ms. Rice went on to make millions as a spokeswoman for a jeans company called No Excuses, which was created to take advantage of just such scandalous events. Gary Hart became a has-been before he had ever been.

I put Sugar Ray Robinson on the canvas—when he tripped over my body.

—Rocky Graziano

If a thing is worth doing, it is worth doing badly.

—G. K. Chesterton

**It's pretty sad when a person has to lose weight to play Babe Ruth.**

—John Goodman

Sports have often been described as the highest form of human endeavor. However, once Dame Fortune takes a hand in the proceedings, any tour de force endeavor rapidly becomes a tour de farce. Relay batons are dropped, vaulting poles snap, riding saddles slip, and diving boards break—all while the crowds roar and the cameras roll. Here are a few athletes who will live on in infamy:

According to the writer Tacitus, a Greek spectator named Effocles became the first recorded track-and-field casualty when a javelin was hurled with exceptional force. The force was a little too exceptional, as the javelin sped out of the field and into the audience, impaling the hapless Effocles.

After several near-fatal accidents on the track, Giuseppe Farina became the first world champion racing driver by winning the Italian Grand Prix at Monza in 1950. He survived a catalog of racing horror stories and, in 1957, finally retired from the most dangerous sport in the world. Three years later, he was killed in a car crash while traveling to the French Grand Prix.

One good deed may deserve another, but how about one of Murphy's deeds? Richard Specas once attempted to set off 100,000 dominoes and break the world's record. Specas's efforts were thwarted by a television cameraman who was waiting to shoot pictures of the historic moment. Ninety-seven thousand five hundred dominoes had been carefully placed when the cameraman's press badge dropped off his jacket, setting the dominoes crashing prematurely.

Harvey Gartley made his way into the history books by being the first boxer to knock himself out. The novice boxer started promisingly, bobbing and weaving, as did his opponent, Dennis Outlette. Forty-seven seconds into the first round of the Saginaw, Michigan, Golden Gloves contest (with neither boxer actually throwing a punch), Harvey moved in for the kill. He swung mightily, missed, collapsed onto the canvas, and was counted out.

A lady at the Shawnee Invitational for Ladies at Shawnee-on-Delaware, Pennsylvania, made golfing history in 1912 when she took 166 strokes over a 130-yard hole.

A goalkeeper's life is often not a happy one, especially when someone like Brazilian soccer star Roberto Revelino scores one of the fastest goals in history. He was passed the ball from the kickoff and shot at the goal tended by Isadore Irandir of Brazil's Río Preto team. The ball scorched by the kneeling Irandir's ear just as he was finishing his prematch prayers.

Vikings defensive lineman Jim Marshall scored one of the most memorable touchdowns in NFL history, although it was a play Marshall himself would love to forget. He got hold of the ball, and his team hoped for the "big play." As Marshall raced down the field toward the goal line, he couldn't hear the crowd screaming and couldn't see his own teammates desperately trying to tackle him—he could only think of one thing: touchdown. He crossed the end zone and triumphantly spiked the football into the ground. Marshall's victorious moment quickly evaporated when he discovered he had run the wrong way and had just scored for the opposition.

On October 8, 1916, Georgia Tech. beat Cumberland University in football with the record-breaking score of 222 to 0. The most exhausted person in the match was the scorekeeper.

In 1976, Canada hosted the Summer Olympics in Montreal. It was the only time an Olympic host country failed to win any gold medals.

Getting out of bed in the morning is an
act of false confidence.

—Jules Feiffer

A bank is a place where they lend you an
umbrella in fair weather and ask for it back
when it begins to rain.

—Robert Frost

*life stinks*

Nothing is so good as it seems beforehand.

—George Elio

The only way to keep your health is to eat
what you don't want, drink what you don't
like, and do what you'd rather not.

—Mark Twair

ne night during flight training in the navy, I
ad landed my plane without remembering to
ut the wheels down. Except for ruining the
ropeller, it was a beautiful landing that left
ne unscratched. When the plane finally
kidded to a stop in showers of sparks, I
tood up in the cockpit with spotlights playing
ver me while sirens screamed and fire trucks
nd ambulances roared to the scene. Standing
here with my stupidity on brightly lit display
efore the entire squadron, I knew for the
rst time in my life what utter humiliation felt
ke.

—Russell Baker

There was no respect for youth when I was young, and now that I am old, there is no respect for age. I missed it coming and going

—J. B. Priestley

I have the true feeling of myself only when I am unbearably unhappy.

—Franz Kafka

If life was fair, Elvis would be alive and all the impersonators would be dead.

—Johnny Carson

**Hell is—other people!**

> —Jean-Paul Sartre

**It is an ill wind that blows when you leave the hairdresser.**

> —Phyllis Diller

**If my film makes one more person miserable, I've done my job.**

> —Woody Allen

Preparing for the worst is an activity I have taken up since I turned thirty-five, and the worst actually began to happen.

—Delia Ephron

Happiness is an imaginary condition, formerly attributed by the living to the dead, now usually attributed by adults to children, and by children to adults.

—Thomas Szasz

If you live long enough, you'll see that every victory turns into a defeat.

—Simone de Beauvoir

Latent in every man is a venom of amazing bitterness, a black resentment; something that curses and loathes life, a feeling of being trapped, of having trusted and been fooled, of being the helpless prey of impotent rage, blind surrender, the victim of a savage, ruthless power that gives and takes away, enlists a man, drops him, promises and betrays, and—crowning injury—inflicts on him the humiliation of feeling sorry for himself.

—Paul Valéry

I don't know, I don't care, and it doesn't make any difference.

—Jack Kerouac

The basic fact about human existence is not that it is a tragedy, but that it is a bore.

—H. L. Mencken

I figure you have the same chance of winning the lottery whether you play or not.

—Fran Lebowitz

I was the green monkey, the pariah. And I had no friends. Not just a few friends, or one good friend, or grudging acceptance by other misfits and outcasts. I was alone. All stinking alone, without even an imaginary playmate.

—Harlan Ellison

We all live in a house on fire, no fire department to call; no way out, just the upstairs
window to look out of while the fire burns
the house down with us trapped, locked in it.
—Tennessee Williams

Meditate upon exile, torture, wars, diseases,
shipwreck, so that you may not be a novice
to any misfortune.

—Seneca

Misery acquaints a man with strange
bedfellows.

—William Shakespeare

Do you know how helpless you feel if you have a full cup of coffee in your hand and you start to sneeze?

—Jean Kerr

The secret of being miserable is to have the leisure to bother about whether you are happy or not.

—George Bernard Shaw

Submit to the present evil, lest a greater one befall you.

—Phaedrus

Success and failure are both difficult to endure. Along with success come drugs, divorce, fornication, bullying, travel, medication, depression, neurosis, and suicide. With failure comes failure.

—Joseph Heller

The text of this book
is set in Matrix, Electrix,
and La Bamba, by M space,
Brooklyn, New York.
Book design by
Maura Fadden Rosenthal.

One day Puss heard that
the King was preparing
to take a drive by the
river with his daughter,
the beautiful Princess.

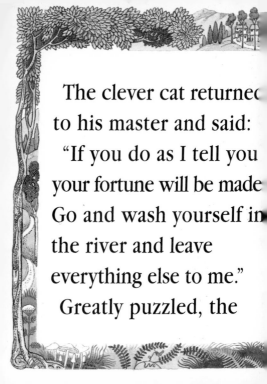

The clever cat returned
to his master and said:
"If you do as I tell you
your fortune will be made.
Go and wash yourself in
the river and leave
everything else to me."
Greatly puzzled, the

oung man did as he was
old. He went down to
he river, undressed and
aded into the water.
While he was washing
e heard the clatter of
orses' hooves coming
loser along the road.

Soon the King passed
by in his coach. At once
the cat began to cry out:

"Help! help! My Lord
Marquis of Carabas is
drowning! Help! Help!"

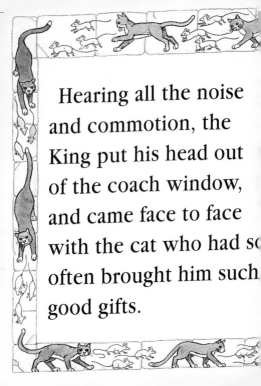

Hearing all the noise and commotion, the King put his head out of the coach window, and came face to face with the cat who had so often brought him such good gifts.

Quickly, the King
commanded his foot-
men to help his Lordship,
the Marquis of Carabas.
In they waded in all
their finery and pulled
the poor Marquis out of
the river. Then Puss

told the King that while his Master was washing, some rogues had stolen all his clothes

But what the cunning cat had really done was hide the clothes under a great big stone. For he

realised that his young
master could not possibly
meet the King dressed in
such shabby attire.

The King immediately
commanded his servants
to run to the Palace and
fetch a selection of his
best suits for the Lord
Marquis of Carabas.

When he was dressed
in his fine new clothes,

the cat's master made a
most impressive figure.
The Princess secretly
thought him the most
handsome man she had

ever seen, and he was
equally taken with her.

As they were introduced
he could not help but
look at her tenderly and
in a trice the Princess
had fallen in love. The
King invited the young
man to join them in the
coach and soon he found

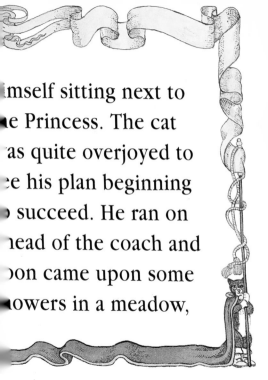

mself sitting next to
e Princess. The cat
as quite overjoyed to
e his plan beginning
 succeed. He ran on
ead of the coach and
on came upon some
owers in a meadow,

busy at work with their scythes. Scowling fiercely, the cat spoke to them.

"Good people, the King is heading this way. If you do not tell him that the meadow you mow

belongs to my Lord
Marquis of Carabas, you
shall be chopped as small
as herbs for the pot."

Along came the King
and, asking his coachman
to stop, he leaned out of
the window and spoke
to the mowers.

"Good people," he said. "This is a lush meadow. To whom does this fine field belong?"

"To my Lord Marquis of Carabas," they all replied together, for the cat's threats had made

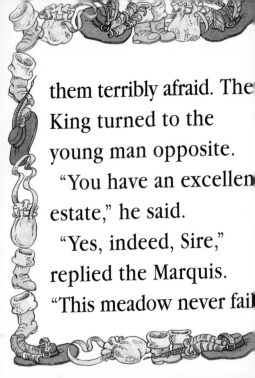

them terribly afraid. The
King turned to the
young man opposite.

"You have an excellen
estate," he said.

"Yes, indeed, Sire,"
replied the Marquis.
"This meadow never fai

give me a plentiful
harvest each year."
Meanwhile Master Puss,
running ahead of the
coach, met some men
reaping a field of corn.
"Good people," he said.
The King is heading this

way. If you do not tell
him that all this corn
belongs to the Marquis
of Carabas, you shall be
chopped as small as
herbs for the pot."

The King, who passed by a moment later, was indeed curious to know who owned such a splendid field of corn.

"It is my Lord Marquis of Carabas," replied the reapers, and the King

as very impressed and
gain congratulated the
Iarquis on his fine land.
And so they continued
n their way. The cat
an ahead of the coach
nd warned each and
very person he met

that they should tell the King the same story. And so they did until the King was quite astonished by the vast estates of the Lord Marquis of Carabas.

"Almost as large as my own," he thought.

Soon Master Puss came
to a magnificent castle.
Now he had taken great
care to discover all he
could about the master
of this castle. He knew
that he was an ogre and,
what is more, the riche

gre in all the land —
d it was he who owned
l the fine estates through
hich the King had
en driven.

The cat marched
raight up to the huge
stle and called out:

"Oh, Master Ogre! I could not pass so close to your fine castle without having the honour of paying my respects."

The ogre was flattered by this little speech and, in as polite a manner as

was possible for such a
fierce creature, he
invited Puss inside.

"I have heard," said the
cat, "that you have magic

powers. I have been told
that you have the gift of
being able to change
yourself into any sort of
creature you want. Is it
true that you can turn
yourself into a lion, or
an elephant?"

"That is true," answered the ogre proudly, "and if you don't believe me, watch this!"

With a flash and a bang, there stood a huge lion! Opening his jaws wide, the creature let out a fierce roar.

Puss was so terrified
that he shot out of the
window and climbed
up onto the roof. There
his boots caused him n
end of trouble, for they
slipped and slid over the
shiny tiles and more

nan once he nearly fell
o his death. From the
oom below him came
he sound of laughing
nd, feeling a little
oolish, the cat climbed
own and scrambled in
hrough the window.

"I must admit," he told the ogre, "that I was scared out of my wits by your ferocious lion. I would not have believed such a thing possible had I not seen it with my own eyes."

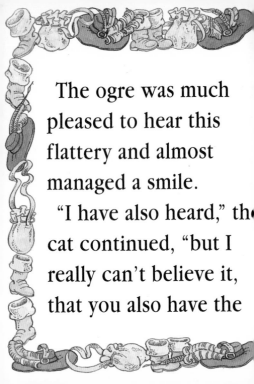

The ogre was much pleased to hear this flattery and almost managed a smile.

"I have also heard," the cat continued, "but I really can't believe it, that you also have the

ower to take on the
shape of the smallest
animals. For example, I
have heard you can
change yourself into a
rat or a mouse, but I
have to say I think that
would be impossible."

"Impossible?" cried the
ogre. "Just watch this!"
And with a flash and a
bang he changed himself
into a mouse and began
to run about the floor.

Straightaway clever Puss
pounced on him with
his sharp claws and ate
him up in one bite.

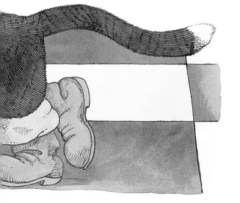

And so, with the ogre gone
for good, the cunning
Puss succeeded in
winning for his master
the finest castle in all
the land.

Meanwhile the Royal
coach was approaching.

81

The King was curious to know who lived in such a splendid place. When Puss heard the rumble of his Majesty's coach crossing the bridge, he ran out and bowed before the King

"Your Majesty is most welcome at this castle, home of my Lord Marquis of Carabas," he said. "What! My Lord Marquis," cried the King, "so this fine castle also belongs to you! What a beautiful courtyard! What magnificent buildings! I should very much like to take a closer look."

And so the King entered
the castle, followed by
his daughter, who held
the Marquis by the hand.

They walked into a huge
hall and there spread
before them was a
splendid banquet, for the
ogre had been expecting
visitors that very day and
had prepared a special
feast. The cat scurried

hither and thither as he
served the royal guests
and the Marquis behaved
all the while as if he had
always been a noble Lord!

As the meal drew to an
end, the King, who had
drunk five or six glasses

of the ogre's best wine,
felt very contented. He
had been watching my
Lord Marquis of Carabas

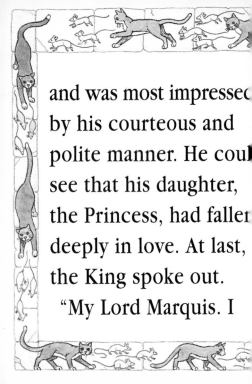

and was most impressed
by his courteous and
polite manner. He coul
see that his daughter,
the Princess, had faller
deeply in love. At last,
the King spoke out.

"My Lord Marquis. I

ve been most pleased
 all that I have seen
day. I would like to
fer you the honour of
coming my son-in-law
d, if you don't accept,
en you will only have
urself to blame."

The Marquis could
hardly believe his ears.
He looked at the Princess
and, blushing with
pleasure, she smiled back
happily. The clever cat
was so pleased that his
plan had finally worked

and he had won for his
master all the riches an
happiness his heart cou
ever desire, that he
scampered out into the
courtyard and performe
fourteen cartwheels
straight off! And so the

arquis of Carabas and
e Princess were married
at very same day.
'uss was made a noble
ord, and never again
d to chase after mice
- well, only when he
ncied some fun!

## CHARLES PERRAULT

*Puss in Boots* first appeared in print in
1697 in the collection of fairy stories written
by the French poet and storyteller,
Charles Perrault (1628-1703).

The collection brought together many
half-forgotten traditional folk tales, including
*Bluebeard*, *Little Red Riding-Hood* and
*Cinderella* and together they became known
as *Mother Goose's Tales*. Written in a simple,
unaffected style, Perrault's stories quickly
became popular in France and later
throughout the world.

There has been considerable dispute
over the years as to the exact author of these
tales and some experts believe that it was
actually Perrault's son, Pierre (1678-1700)
who compiled and recorded the stories for
posterity when he was only 17 or 18 years old.